SHORELESS

Shoreless

POEMS

Enid Shomer

A Karen & Michael Braziller Book
PERSEA BOOKS / NEW YORK

Persea Books, Inc.
90 Broad Street
New York, New York 10004

Library of Congress Cataloging-in-Publication Data

Names: Shomer, Enid, author.
Title: Shoreless : poems / Enid Shomer.
Description: New York : A Karen & Michael Braziller Book/Persea Books, [2020] |
    Summary: "In Shoreless, winner of the 2019 Lexi Rudnitsky Editor's Choice Award, Enid
    Shomer continues to explore her passionate relationship with the Florida landscape, the
    inextricable web of family, and the challenges of the body. While studded with the austere
    recognitions of growing older, these poems are punctuated by humor and play-formally
    elegant and inventive, beautifully textured and nuanced. Throughout the book, Shomer
    employs the language of science and Eros to uncover the exquisite truths of pain and
    pleasure—Provided by publisher.
Identifiers: LCCN 2020024083 | ISBN 9780892555215 (paperback)
Subjects: LCGFT: Poetry.
Classification: LCC PS3569.H5783 S56 2020 | DDC 811/.54—dc23
LC record available at https://lccn.loc.gov/2020024083

Book design and composition by Rita Lascaro
Typeset in Palatino
Manufactured in the United States of America. Printed on acid-free paper.

Again, for L. T.

CONTENTS

But as in landlessness alone resides the highest truth, shoreless, indefinite as God—so, better is it to perish in that howling infinite, than be ingloriously dashed upon the lee, even if that were safety! For worm-like, then, oh! who could craven crawl to land!

HERMAN MELVILLE, *MOBY DICK*

Right at the heart of my ability to grasp the truth, I want to be paralyzed, I want to swoon . . . I want my mind to fail before the truth. I want the truth to flow over me only as something sensual and as nothing else.

DENIS JOHNSON, *TREE OF SMOKE*

I.

PINK LIGHT

Rara Omnia

If there's life after death, it isn't the body
I'd want, which after all is a rather shoddy
container. I'd want to come back as pure voice.

I'd want to tell of this beach before the turtles
confused the porch lights for moons as they hurtled
ashore to lay their eggs. I wouldn't point

an accusing finger. I just want the record
straight, to tell how black skimmers in sinuous hordes
turned in the sky like pages of print; how they strained

the sea, their lower mandibles seining for fish.
That the snowy plovers took flight in waves of applause,
their wings beating so fast they seemed to pause,

strobe-lit. I'd tell how the sea relents
in early spring, exposing the muck where creatures spend
themselves in extravagant numbers—fighting conchs

hopping like slow rabbits in search of a mate
on their singular black feet; Atlantic cockles in spate,
their speckled mantles like pink tongues on which

they twirl and fall through the inch-deep surf
in a ritual dance. And skates dragging a scarf
through the shallows as their wingtips

and eye ridges froth the water to tulle.
And horse conchs, with their glossy orange lips
cartwheeling over the sand bar, heroic

as salmon swimming upstream. Then the water stood
still—limpid, glassed out, afloat with ripe
coconuts and mangrove pods, those brown-tipped

exclamations, each an infant tree that accretes
an island if given a toehold. For weeks
the tides lay like a blanket over the freshly laid

eggs—the leathery leis of the lightning whelk,
the castanets of conchs with dozens of baby
gastropods inside each disk of salty milk.

At the end of a month, the water peeled back
like bells ringing, and everywhere the egg sacs
burst, and tiny offspring poured forth.

This was before the beach became a catcher's mitt
for trash, before the oil spills and red tides,
before the hard corals blanched and died,

before the fire sponges rotted in their red glory.
If I could come back I'd tell this story and the stories
found only in record books: the tarpon reaching

twelve feet, the groupers big as cars,
cone shells grown heavy as bricks on their packs
of poison harpoons. And everywhere the fish, scarce

now—mackerel, trout, pompano, drum—so
plentiful once they fed us for millennia.
I'd send my voice like a whale song into the deep

threading it through turtle grass and sea wrack
singing to the soft corals and sea hares, the polychete
worms and squid, *Come back if you can, come back.*

White Ibises

The sea unfurls them
from its carpet of blue,
white bodies feathered

with surf, the red feet
and beak coughed up
from the deep

of dreams. The bill begins
its work. Foraging by touch
the elegant curve reaches

into crab holes, probes
the shingle for coquinas,
those tiny clams closed shut

like butterfly wings at rest.
All day as they hunt, the ibises print
the Hebrew letters *ayin*

and *sheen* in the sand,
whole alphabets the waves roll
into sacred scrolls that hold up

the world. The waves crest ceaselessly.
The birds write on till dusk
when, high in the sky, they pass

for clouds, their black-tipped wings
the leading edge
of thunderheads in the rainy

payment the sky renders
the sea for bearing them again
each morning.

On St. George Island

Four years since I've touched this water
or pulled out a fish or lain on my back
at the lip of the tidal zone awaiting

the Gulf's crisp white patter,
the serious blue ideas that take me
far into myself, as in love,

and then far out, as in love. Salt
spray like a day-old beard stings
and scratches, relaxes into old

lace. The surf's attentive to crease
and pore, a lover who traded his temper
today for extra hands. Like a fountain

pen left to leak while a thought
coheres, it inks my suit in deltas
of Lycra, fiber by fiber. It opens

the dark fan of my hair, pries me
from where the purple-winged coquinas
flutter, releasing pearls of air,

and floats me on its endless hand
until I'm washing back and forth,
clear daughter of the tides.

The Pink Light

In late summer, the pink light of Florida
dusk descends, a tint I imagine the Impressionists
would have liked. And perhaps it shines
in Provence, but I've never seen it anywhere else—
not in Tel Aviv or Istanbul, Athens, Paris,
or Jerusalem. For forty minutes stones blush
like flesh, water assumes a violet hue,
and the trees turn bluish as in old Technicolor film.
The pink light suffuses everything: natural
rose-colored glasses, a visual blessing.

Today at dusk I recalled with admiration
a friend who'd admitted to her own small moral
failings. Her lover had been in the hospital
and the doctors weren't paying her enough attention.
So, she began to brag about the lover—
"She has a PhD in Neurobiology, has published
papers"—setting her apart from—and above—
the mostly poor unschooled patients on the ward.
In other words, trying to convince the doctors
she was more worth saving.

It's hard work to ponder one's moral
failings. Like seeing through the pink light,
where everything looks more beautiful,
they seem egregious by contrast—a dash of blood
in a porcelain basin, a touch of rot
on an apricot. So let's begin with a question:
why was I such a mandarin earlier,
name-dropping exotic cities as if
I were a well-traveled aesthete and you,

my precious reader, a lowly plebe.
If that isn't a moral failing, it's the start

of one. And now, confessing it, perhaps
to stir up sympathy and complicity.
Or your awe. My friend's lover recovered,
but who can say what effect her comments had?

And how bad does she feel about it?
"It took me a long time to figure out
what I'd done," she said. Would you
do it again? I asked. "Yes," she said,
"I think I might."

Rara Avis

Charadrius alexandrinus

What will become of the snowy plover?
Only two hundred mating pairs remain.
Tiny shore birds, they lay their eggs over

a divot of sand at the wrack line, without cover,
reduced by the smallest foot to a yellow stain.
What will become of the snowy plover

that little puff of a party favor,
the perfect pocket-pet if it could be tamed?
These tiny shore birds lay their eggs over

the same scrapes in the sand despite beach lovers
spreading their towels, unaware and without blame.
What will become of the snowy plover,

its legs black straws that blur like wind-up levers
imprinting the shore with a chevron chain.
Such tiny birds, they lay their eggs over

this beach by instinct, unable to adjust a sliver,
not knowing what they risk, or what must be reclaimed.
Endangered means that I feel the grief the plover
can't as it lays its eggs in the sand over and over.

Driving through the Animal

Through my window, the buzz of a distant combine
cutting a swath through the far pasture of rye,
small animals caught in its wheeling blades—
rabbits shived to wet ribbons, field mice
reduced to minims of bloody fur as the field
flattens into the lush avenues of our hungers.

At drivers' school last Fall I learned it's a fatal
mistake to spare the deer, possum or pet
in the road. Drive *through* the animal, the officer
said. Since flesh gives, collision—even
with a steer—is safer than a wild swerve
into oncoming traffic, culvert, or tree.

I know how it happens: past midnight near Cedar Key,
the road cinching up on its yellow thread.
Star-bright eyes cluster like low constellations.
I drive through the herd, the car my armor,
telling myself they're only a thicket of bone
and blood. Like faint quarter moons, hooves rise

in my headlights, a body slams—brief trophy—
on the grille. Deer often die of fright
before they die of their wounds. But mine casts
in the road for hours, its tongue spilled, flies
working the open spots, vultures sifting
down from trees. The truth is I'd never drive

straight through. Whatever it is that leaps
in my chest would become what leapt in the road.

Pool Party

Far to the west
lightning pins corsages
of clouds on the night
sky. These are reflected
in the canal like cheap
special effects.
Everyone points
and waits for the thunder
which never comes.

The host tells an anecdote:
Thirty parrots she had.
That's when I took up
whiskey as a profession.
His second wife smooths
her skirt. Their pet
bulldog whines, dragging
the chair it's tied to
across the patio.

Above, Orion takes aim.
Parrot jokes erupt, the wife
laughing as if she were a chime
played by the wind.
If I look away from the clouds
grouted with silver, I see her
trembling hands
and the new pool I came to swim in—
a gash in their land.

Aubade with Herons

Awake again, calculating my lack of sleep,
I hear their feathers sift into place. No help

from the pills slogged down, the milk swirled
with cinnamon into a spiral I hoped to curl

inside. It's sleeping alone that hurts. In the atlas
of my sleep, you're the shore and I'm the wave that laps—

when I throw a leg over your leg
or our hands lie clasped like a lock on the cage

of our chests. Only touch could spoon me back
into the bottle of sleep, lift me over the lake

edged with herons, into the trees pastelled
by painted buntings the month before you left.

Jazz at Bradley's

Between sets the brass swan
sleeps propped against a wall
long neck drinking in the darkness
that must be swallowed to make a song

digress from melody until
the veins on the players' necks bulge
like conduits, the left hand sasses
the right on the ivories, and the drums

race to a stop like long-jumpers
churning through air.
I heard this music once before,
canoeing the Suwannee—willow leaves

dropping like mallets on patches of water
bright as the slats of a vibraphone,
beavers gnawing branches down
to motes swirling like the galaxies

of secondhand smoke above this bar
whose patrons slump, oblivious
with pleasure as the drummer hoists a harness
of sleighbells and shakes it, once.

Shoreless

I want to be like water, go low where there
is least resistance, loll in the vestibules
of leaks, the flaws of casks, painlessly pool
around rocks, unworried about which part
of me splits off. I want to flow, drop
by drop, with crown-shaped splatters, hang
like a spangled globule on the oily feather
of a bird, jewel-like in the sun, or be flung

in diamond-crested shakes by a wet dog.
Let me be of a piece, the shape of shape-
lessness, like my airy partner, the fog.
Let me forget I'm caught in the trap
of a body, that abyss of bone and blood
inside my skin where I founder, drowning.

Survival in the Thirteenth Year

Today, instead of writing
an ode to my breasts
before they were cut
and irradiated like food
to extend their shelf life,
I gather a branch of nickernut,
its ferocious spiked pods
and thorny canes reminders
that life can be vicious.
I like the way the nickernut
or warri tree scrambles
over other shrubs to grow
in impenetrable thickets
a few yards from the sea,
draping the beach
with the spiny cape of a giant.

I touch the coral bean's
lipstick-shaped blooms
on three-foot-long racemes
that could be tail feathers
of a huge flame-colored bird.
And the square-stemmed nosegay
of scarlet sage, and the gopher tortoise
shell with its hollow sockets.

Nature feels like a friendship
the world offers. Miraculous
we are all here: the wildflowers
in their magical diversity,
me abiding like a wind-stunted
tree. Even the lowly plantain weed

charms, its soft green leaves
like spatulas smoothing the edge

of the path where I walk,
the sun on my neck as I pass
rattlebox's yellow flowers
and dowdy Spanish needle
and other blooms so small
they have no common names,
though in the body they'd be large
deadly sites, labeled and staged.

II.

A WEIGHTLESS EMBRACE

From Whom the Evening Flows

The Nazirites, those old Jews
in the Bible who offered God their uncut
hair and were forbidden wine

and funerals, considered night
not absence or blight but an arrival—
shadows tucking boulders back

into a field, a cape alluding
to luscious shoulders. While the green
world breathes, the stars burn

like ascetics, their fiery tresses invisible
in the day against a sky I can't
avoid calling heaven, the dome

of the toyed-with world wrought from Nothing.
The old trick of the sun seeming
to sink and rise disappears

in the Hebrew, which names God "the eveninger
of evenings"—a phrase irreducible
as the brute equality of graveyards.

Whatever keeps us, we can only
praise that steep idea, the whatever-
it-is that brings the dark from which

the dreamer wakes and harks.

The Brain

Not the aorta which had burst,
or the feet which splayed out
lending a slightly clownish stance.
Not the hair, that cloud of silver wishes.
What they wanted was the brain.
Before the body was cremated,
Dr. Thomas Harvey secretly
removed it, along with the eyes—
a gift to the great man's ophthalmologist.

Harvey measured the brain forty
different ways, perfused it
with formalin and took dozens
of black-and-white photos
from unusual angles—science *noir*.
He sectioned it into 240 cubes.
Wrapped in white gauze, they resembled
chunks of Turkish Delight.
For nearly fifty years, wherever he moved,

he took the brain with him, stored
in two glass apothecary jars,
while he waited for science to advance.
Because the brain began to fold in
on itself when homo sapiens
first evolved, it wasn't surprising
that *above all*, Harvey noted,
the brain looked human.
But Einstein had more prefrontal

cortical ridges than usual—four
instead of three in each hemisphere—
leaving lots of room
for speculation. Was this the anatomy
of genius, or were these extra ridges
no more significant than the skull
bumps phrenologists used to predict character?
And what of love? Where was its neuroanatomy—
the place where sensory deprivation
carves its scars?

The brain was slightly smaller
than average with more glial cells,
and in 2012, when Harvey's photos
were released, a knob was found,
present in all who study the violin
from a young age. When stuck
on a physics problem, Einstein played
the fiddle. Some say music enabled him

to watch gravity bend,
space curve, time slow down.
If only we could have scanned
his prefrontal cortex while he lived,
observed the parietal lobes glowing
as he pondered space / time
or a bunch of carrots for dinner.

So far we know that the brain is an organ
that develops out of love. Love
of another, love of the way light
rouges the backlit earlobe

or sets the hair aflame, love
of the night sky, of the way two
trains passing each other
in a station appear to stand still.

Milkweed

In late afternoon light with the tang
of cider, we watch as shadows drape
the landscape with stateliness. Below,
the figured carpet of the valley darkens.
Behind us, in a sunlit pasture, cattle
switch their tails, dusting up chowdery
swirls of milkweed silk.

A stranger to nature-inspired bliss,
you wait in the car while an hour disappears
into the great variety—pods
like hollow talons smelling of split wood,
dimpled green blimps packed with white
satin parachutes, each filament
the sail for a seed.

When we fell in love, you asked to look
at parts of me I'd never seen myself.
I burned with modesty. Later, your gaze
was thrilling, a kind of weightless embrace,
like the way you stared at your own paintings—
leisurely and full of wonderment.

The stalks I'm harvesting to mash into
handmade paper lean together on the fence.
Beyond them, I see you have followed me
into the field like a lover undressing after
his partner. Crouched in the grass, you plunder pod
after pod, orange ladybugs thronging
your hands as you spin the white stars
on the plume of your breath.

Vow

My sidecar, my silver spoon,
perfect curl of pencil shaving.
Smooth volute. Dangle dude.
Fine cheroot, the beard of bees
between my legs. Fix me a highball.

Give me all your transitive verbs.
Loyal and loving, I daven your name.
I'm gutta-percha holding on
by the roots, a marabou fan tenderizing
your thighs. Through radiance and filth,

through blubbering grief and parabolas
of rage, through age, I swear on this chorus
of sequined girls jazzed on
amphetamines and performing deep
salaams, you're mine.

Lightning Demonstration

Museum of Science, Boston

In a hushed and darkened
room, with preschoolers so wired they threaten
to emit sparks,

spotlights fall
on what Dr. Frankenstein rigged to call
the life force from the sky:

Van de Graaff
generators, flinging forty-foot gaffs
barbed with light.

A sizzling arcade
fetches up in the blackness; tree-shapes fade
to twigs intaglioed

on our retinas in red
sealing wax. Here Thor and Zeus were bred,
all the gods of promise and fear.

Our guide enters
a cage and ascends through the ozone-rich, rent
air. Science

solid as a lag-bolt
is the shield he wears while thirty million volts
ransack his prison

licking through the bars
for tinder or flesh to ignite. He wouldn't dare
such a feat without

knowing the laws
that insulate him from the fiery claws
of the lightning and keep

the rest of us safe.
The certainties of science outweigh faith.
As the lightning climbs

the machine's spiral
rods, popping like hot champagne bubbles
I am awed but not

afraid, while the children shriek
a delight streaked
with panic until

the guide unlocks
and exits his sleeve of steel, not a mock
god, but a man

who has survived
a miracle, who is alive
by virtue of smarts.

An unexpected sound
like lightbulbs fizzling out
floats up in the vault—

the children's scattered applause.

On the Ramp of the Brooklyn Bridge

Carefully picking his way
across black ice, a man offers
to wash the windshield. Have I seen him before?
Is it the dirt-colored clothes
I recognize, or my own fear?
His stocking cap, navy with melting flakes,
sparkles like a universe
as he intersects the head beams and waves
a stiffened rag.

Not enough ammonia, he explains,
when the spritz bottle freezes.
Glances dart between us
like startled birds. He rattles
a paper cup with seed
money brought from home,
that lean-to city under the fretwork
where fires in oil drums
bloody the girders, and men sleep

huddled together. Not like a pride
of lions, that relaxed loving
pile of ligament
and mane, not like a line resting
before it worms forward in a suppressed surge,
but like a heap of clothes
in the giveaway pile
as the snow falls around them
painting them out of its pristine path.

Walking Home at Dusk in a New City

I'm trying to be grateful for my new life,
but thinking of Keats, imagining a movie
of his last months. I want him to enter
the Victorian age, recite his odes
to decorous crowds, lose his Cockney bray.
But he worsens at twenty-five, his lungs

moth-eaten lace, his face an extinguished lamp.
To salve the pain he applies tincture
of Italian sunlight, the calm-browed
temples of Rome. But he's lonely,
for the mother and brother who died
before him, for the fiancée he never touched

between the legs. Isn't that the beautiful thing
about us—that we're mortal?
At the end of my film Keats climbs
the steps to his flat, running
out of breath at the landing. These days
almost no one succumbs to TB,

though a broken life still heals
slowly. The stairs to my attic apartment lap
at the door like the stylized sea
in a Japanese print. And—Keats could have made
something of this—they're scuffed on the lip
of each tread. Genius, unrequited lover,

my poor hero Keats! The movie ends
before the stairs can be transformed
into anything, leaving earnest oak
scooped out where all the tenants
before me have stood,
fumbling for the key.

Translation

My friend is phoning overseas again
as he has every night since the bombing began.
The way he clutches the receiver
reminds me of the way as a child
I was taught to carry scissors—not by the handles
but by the blades, so the danger
pointed at the palm of my hand
instead of my heart.
Everything is fine,
               considering.
Except tonight his mother
tells a story. I hear him repeat "brain"
and "young" and "sorry." The words
swim around in my head, trying to school
into something that will flash
like a big silver blade. "Don't tell me yet,"
I whisper, stepping outside
to breathe in the sky, disconnect
the stars in the hunter, the hunted.

The End of the Romance

Take away the slow jazz, her silk
dress that stirs color into every
breath, his weight-bearing tweed. Also,
the long sigh of landscape in the windows.
Put the pair back, please, in the cave,
with its drafty passageways and dank walls.
Put animal skins on their bodies,
bear grease in their hair and the dried blood
of the kill under their nails. Nights, let them
tremble at the stealth of predators. Let them
come to it without ritual of shank bone
and feather, no throw of the shaman's
rattle or drinking of tears.
Let them come to it in fear.

Pausing on a Hillside in Anatolia

I've learned to pause from time to time
in this landscape riddled with antiquity
where the hills have swallowed whole cities
and telltale ruins poke from every slope.
Exposed stones like rows
of erupting teeth mean walls
or roads; columns—whether stubs
or towering trunks—mark temples
to Artemis.
     So when the sound begins

in the distance, so faint at first I mistake it
for leaves spooling in the breeze, I stop
and wait, I feel it shiver the hair
on my arms. It grows louder, from the jingle
of coins in an army of pockets to nuggets
of ore riding the rim of a prospector's pan,
shells churning in surf,
the furious tinkling of icicles
in a storm.
     I used to pause like this,

feeling *called*, when the college carillon
tolled at dusk, hurrying me
to my room. Not when it dragged and shuffled
through popular tunes, but the classic dirges,
pedaled *sostenuto*. How
perfectly those giant chimes
heralded the night, spreading
a pall on the air where I heard what I often
felt in my heart—
     how wide is the gulf

between speech and silence, how sad our thoughts,
forever caught between. Now
a goatherd appears with his goats, a patchwork
of grays and browns that billows down
the knoll, the bells on their necks resounding,
bronze and brass, copper and tin
clappers and cups, large as apples
for rams, thimble-sized for kids,
each with its own timbre and pitch.

Later, at the covered bazaar
in Istanbul, at the weekly market
in Tiré, I will try to buy the music,
hefting and sorting bells by shape
and size, but nothing will match these starbursts
of sound, the echoing of this mountain-
sized marimba, glitter spilling
from a vial, rain plinking into hollow
clay jars.
　　　　The herd advances,

leapfrogging toward an ancient stone
trough where they lower their heads to drink,
damping the bells. When they raise them again,
the accidental music resumes—
a xylophone pelted by hail. It covers
me completely, a blanket woven
of thrums and spangles, glissando trills,
the tinsel of tambourines and finger
cymbals.
　　　　Sometimes when I sang

in choir, I felt the bones of my skull
buzzing, music passing through them
like drone strings, my own voice
inaudible in the rainbow of sound
we hung from the rafters. I had to hold hands
with the girl beside me for the highest
soprano riffs, I was so dizzy
with the bliss of blending in.
        Slaked, the caravan

retreats, dragging the sound behind it
like a ninetails of soda cans
and flatware lashed to a newlywed's bumper.
Then, like a siren dopplered by distance,
the pitch drops and fades. I step
forward, straining through the new
silence for any whisper, but even
their hooves fall like felt on the stone
outcrops.
        Years ago, I read

The Lives of the Romantic Poets
and recall now their favorite toy
and metaphor for the poet: the Aeolian
harp, a kind of fretless guitar
placed in a window where gusting breezes
strummed a pensive music that came
from nature, not art. Anyone,
said Shelley, could coax the world to sing,
as today the goats did,
        exchanging

their breath and movement for that celestial
glockenspiel, an alchemy
profound as turning lead to gold.
Far away, the goats run
still, taking their music wherever
they go. Shelley believed the poet
is like the wind harp, and life
the wind that plucks his harmonies,
his poems.
　　　　　Well I have lived in a punishing wind

for years now, but how many bells
could I summon? Never enough for the century's
slaughter. Not even enough to forge
the iron of my own losses into a sounding
shape. After the goats sang
to me in my language, I asked myself how
I could live without that sound, though later
it faded. Later, I could not even
remember their music
　　　　　　　without this poem.

III.

THE CASUAL DECAY OF STARS

How Could I Know

at forty I'd walk with a cane and a tiny
dog wearing a dog slicker on Broadway,

that sometimes I'd give the beggar at the Food
Emporium more than I can afford

and sometimes want to shovel him into a ditch,
that my leg would seem to fill with silt, then switch

off and on like a toy run by remote control,
that I'd leave my beloved Florida for cold

sunsets in a sky like an old gray sheet
and smart alecks who ask if Sonnet,

my dog, is Petrarchan. On x-rays and MRIs
slapped onto light boxes, pain hides

in white caves, forcing my back front and center,
a spoiled brat demanding all my attention,

a wagon wheel with splintered spokes.
I am the cargo it bears upstairs, the *pack*

in *pack animal*, the *dope* in *all doped up*.
I've got the foot with *foot drop*,

collapsible as my cane which unfolds all at once
with a series of clicks befitting a tap dance.

I used to tap. I used to play varsity
basketball, broke my ankle in the city

championships and never warmed the bench.
Which is to say I didn't know an inch

from a mile, didn't know a thing that had broken
might never mend.

Luminous Flux

Riding a narrow bed, I enter a tube
lit like a harbor tunnel—cool fluorescence

on white tiles, my body limned with glare.
I shut my eyes, invoke the tang,

the pucker and drool of words
like *sour pickle, chalk, ginger root.* . . .

Even fish suffer: it has been proved.
Whatever is sensate. Materially speaking,

death is a power outage. Some believe
afterward the soul keeps on shining

like a beam of light switched to the invisible ends
of the spectrum where x-rays and radio waves

reveal unhealed fractures, tumors, the casual
decay of stars, quarks emitting notes

like whale songs from the vast oceans,
and, hypothetically, even ghosts, which flicker

in and out of visibility. But now, light etches
its prophecy on film, a shape resembling

a tiny nebula, the exhaust chuffed out at bus
terminals. The patient exits, hoisting herself

like a gymnast over a pommel horse, or a horse
clearing a fence, the fence (like the woman) existing

in time and space as something *between*—meadow
and road, mount and ground, date and date.

It's all a matter of scale: rights of way
versus cellular margins, the moon above

and the lunular moons at the base of the nails.
Still, I have always hated sleep.

Three Disks, Two Rods, and a Dozen Screws

A week before circumferential fusion with hardware,
the masseuse places the blade of her hand on my spine,
murmuring *Close your eyes and imagine flakes*
of metal swirling like snow. Flurries of iron

drift down from I-beams and trestles, stick
to my skin like filings to a magnet, then pass
painlessly through, forming a subcutaneous
armor so my resolve won't flicker,

so there's a wick in the candle of my flesh,
so I can toss aside my canes and stand
strong as a bronze horse that rears while
his general hangs his hat on the sky, that grows

greener, more fervent in storms—huge hollow
body flying on armature, as mine will
once the surgeons implant the titanium, the steel.

Villanelle for My Two Spines

O chain of bones, you venomous snake
articulating like a rusty hinge,
I arched with pleasure before you ached

like a rotten tooth, a lip snagged on a fishhook.
I saw the surgeons' implements arranged
before I slept in my chain of bones. They cut the snake

at the lumbar curve. Scalpels trailed a wake
of scars; inside, the nerves inflamed. I binged
on pills that gave no pleasure, failed to quell the ache.

The last resort: doctors using titanium disks,
steel rods and screws, implanted a cage
around the chain of bones. Now the venomous snake

lives within this scaffold, its bionic
twin. Held as still as fluid in a syringe,
it gives a zero-sum pleasure: the slackening

of pain. Will the old spine slip its bars and attack?
Or will the new one with its duller twinges
reign? O chain of bones, you venomous snake
I'll settle for this pleasure: a back with a bearable ache.

Lying In Bed, Visualizing Bone Growing

Objects bob up from the blue well
in my arm where every shift the nurses fill

syringes: my father's tackle box, its findings
corroded to junk; the necklaces I popped

apart in Woolworth's that time they called the cops;
an ankle bracelet engraved *You're my everything,*

Love, Pete. The morphine pump delivers.
By the bed, American Beauty roses run

like wet paint, while singing like the Seven
Dwarves, the tiny workers I've invented

descend my spine with mortar and trowel to lay
calcium bricks. This is the way I pray

to my god, Science, which holds that the mind rules
the soma, an ill-understood remote-control

machine. Thus, yogis flourish in chambers containing
a thimble of air, and deep in trances shamans

solder broken bones while hypnotized
for surgery, Chinese patients, wide-

eyed and alert, bleed as serenely
as swans float. I'm a skeptic, like Houdini.

I want to know how mind over matter works.
The great illusionist never claimed to skirt

the laws of physics, but after his mother died
at séance after séance, he tried

to raise her, like a faint radio signal from space.
Did he fail because there is no life

after death? Or because he pressed the wrong
tabs in his mind? Maybe nothing

travels past the body's shores—
no soul, no voice—and all we have

of the great unknown is more
within.

First Post-op Visit

Like a secular shroud of Turin, my long cassette
x-ray reveals miracles: not the stigmata
of a god, but implants bright as light, the fata
morgana of a spine. I recall the lobster I dissected
to threads—how soft the flesh was within
the carapace. If humans carried their skeletons
on the outside, would our bones still pellet us
with pain? Would they feel more like armor or skin?

There! The doctor points to some cloudy swirls
on the film. *New bone you've grown in the last six
weeks.* The faint wisps look less like the tusks I've
visualized than an angel's feathery curls
or the fog of breath the doctors sought on a mirror
held to the lips to prove the patient was still alive.

Funerary Tusk

At first you dwell on what isn't depicted:
how the elephant was trussed,
its final agony when the tusk

was gouged from its head. Then you notice
the spirals of luminescence, the way
like a glove the worked ivory softens

and folds the light. In each of three
lunettes, scenes from a lady's life:
her royal birth, the silk banners

that heralded her wedding, the heir
foretold by a lane of mulberry trees
bowed in the wind. The highly-prized

"lace" (actually bone-scarring caused
by disease) stands for the slashing rain
of luckless fate. Carved for an Empress

and her unborn child, its maker
understood that grief deepens
and constricts over time, the way light

here falls onto smaller and smaller
spaces as the tusk tapers the procession
to a single mourner kneeling

at the dead woman's palanquin.
Beyond, the artist has bored a tiny
aperture for you to gaze

upon the ruined splendor—a sapphire
carved in the shape of a woman, completely
deprived of light.

Gowned Waiting

is the name of the room where we sit, clutching
rouge-pink robes with flimsy ties. One patient flips

through fashion mags. Her cubicle door ajar,
another rehearses a script, while two friends,

scheduled together, compare injustices
at work. I'm writing this in my journal, trying

for calm against the terror at hand, this visit
a truce with disease I negotiate twice

a year. A woman enters speaking broken
English, weeping. We understand—tears

are the native idiom here in Gowned Waiting.
Minutes ago, she was swept aboard

the diagnosis express, where everything blurs
like a landscape rushing past, though at the moment

her train creeps so slowly that seconds
freeze, refusing to pass, trapping her

in the instant of discovery, the words
that struck like fangs—*malignant, invasive* . . .

bad. The brochure they gave her—support
groups and hotlines, survivors beribboned in pink—

lists on her lap like a shipwrecked paper boat.
She wants to run the day backwards,

as I did last year. To walk back
out through the clinic door to the subway stop,

to my block, to pause in reverse for the breakfast I grabbed
on the run until I'm standing wreathed with steam

in the morning shower, completely clean.

My Number

The chances in 100 of no recurrence of disease in ten years.

This number replaces all previously issued, *et cetera.*
This number replaces your breast.
My father—a gambler—also clutched numbers to his chest,
but his numbers changed with the jockeys' silks. Better a
scientific estimate than his dumb luck.
After surgery my number—seventy-five—
progresses like miles on an odometer, by ticks.
Chemo and radiation bring eight humbling
points, mouth sores, a scalp like a plucked
chicken, and blood counts so low I'm forbidden kisses.
Side effects are the price of the odds, the glitches
of this number earned like a merit badge in dodged
bullets. One patient tells her beads, one keeps
a rabbit's foot; I hold to eighty-three.

Bald

Cue ball, egg, the handles of tools:
everything wants to be smooth,
then smoother—the newel post worn to satin

by generations rushing up and down
stairs scooped out, thinned
like the bowls of spoons. Even languages

slicken. Without the Barbarian hordes,
and given another millennium,
Latin, with its prickly cases

and moods, would have simplified,
like Chinese, till every word
was good for any part of speech:

I own a dog, I dog the dog,
I have dog breath,
I walk dogly . . .

O the beauties of use—the slow-cooked
patina on ivory pistol grips,
the rounded corners of leather books.

And splendor of splendors,
evolution, that plucked the vulture's
head for dipping in guts unhindered

by plumes. I think of my own lost
hair like that—not as the cost
of killing deadly cells, but a sleek

mutation. Bald beneath my Yankee
blue, I tip my cap to nature's
thrift, to cure.

Letter from the Blue Ridge

In this place of earnest minds and work,
there's a room where we signed our names on the wall,
drew monograms entwining our initials.
Seven years ago, before I got sick.

It's warm for October. Gnats swarm my lunch-
box and bees drift by on streams of scent.
The dairy cows have gone for good.
In their place, grazing steers roll up
their lips like loose silk cuffs to chomp
the Osage oranges, those warty melons
originally called *fruit without beginning or end.*

We dubbed our meetings trysts; sometimes we called
my studio "Hotel California," or "the lab,"
referring to the plants I collected in jars—
pokeberry, honeysuckle, sumac with its carmine
velvet spears. And on the sill, Osage
oranges, their milky sap dissolving the paint.
We never spoke of love, also a fruit

without beginning or end. My breath caught
the last morning when you pointed to the horizon
as we woke, saying, *Look! The mountains
here appear and vanish at will.*

I've peeked into the studio we graffitied:
no evidence of our stay, of the mattress thrown
to the floor, or the wax drips from votives rimming
our lair to ward off mice. No inkling, either,
of what lay ahead—spinal collapse, two years

in bed, body braces, and the terrible self-
ishness of pain—all of which we entered

blamelessly as a couple of lovers walking
into the woods. Or into a room with a view
of mountains in the distance—blue at dusk,
pink at dawn, with firebreaks like healed
incisions. Now I think that what you meant
was not that love can't last if mountains don't,
but that mountains can be moved.

And move. Though today they're simply sunning
themselves, lying sprawled chine to hip,
content. I wanted to write and tell you this,
and that I'm well, I'm well.

IV.

THE OLD EMPIRE

Permanent Waves

From memory, that balloon
that fills and deflates, comes Grandma Minerva's beauty salon

and the flat in back where she lived, a couple of dumpy rooms.
Comes Grandma herself, not figure or face or the songs she hummed

but the bouquet of scents that cloaked her as ermine a queen.
Underneath them all, she told me, Rumanian women

had parts like flowers that released a scent especially
arousing to men. She covered hers with *Maja*,

that perfume with a Spanish dancer swirling a black lace
skirt to her thighs like a matador swinging his cape.

But her hands reeked of solutions and dyes. Across the path
of her fragrant life a long line of befores and afters—

debutantes, Cuban matrons with mustachioed lips—
paged through hairdo magazines, fingered wisps

on color charts, a dozen shades of brunette and blonde.
She burnished their dusty curls with peroxide, penciled in

beauty marks like tiny bullseyes. While facials foamed
and pincurls wound down like clocks, in drifted aromas

from her kitchen—*mamaliga*, knishes, brandied pears.
She loved her work, stood on her feet for forty years,

till the dunes of Miami Beach sprouted a castle, the Hotel
Fontainebleau. Paved with marble, laced with spiral

stairs, it erased the helmet dryers, the manicure trays
where fingers splayed like miniature chorus lines. Today,

where Grandma lay on a chaise as she pondered the *Racing Form*
and watched the waves flattening like a bad perm

dangles a three-storey-tall chandelier, a hair ornament
fit for a hurricane lashing shoreward with natural curls.

Gaudy Reds

It will happen, mother said. Just wait.
I kept busy, gathering sumac
near the woods as she taught me,
red velvet spears atop long stems, lemony note
in salads and stews, also used to cut
the saltiness of anchovy paste on toast.
Some days I set the table with an Amaryllis bulb
forced in a shallow pot, trumpet pledged
to festivity. Other days with hibiscus,
five frilly petals circling stamen and pistil.
It might come stealthily, like the scarlet
tanager I searched for each spring,
red bird with a black fantail that juts like a comb
from the flamenco dancer's hair.

According to ads, eventually someone
would kiss my creamy vermillion lips.
His throat scorched by the ornamental peppers
in my chili, I'd feed him pomegranate seeds.
We were both in love with the taste of blue
ocean in lobsters and crabs, those red-hot
creatures father steamed in a garbage pail
in the backyard. I remember the satisfied
snapping shut of the red patent leather clutch
I carried as a girl. Matching kitten heels.
Over and over I played what I loved:
the red vinyl record of *Black Orpheus,*
until the gaudiness I waited for showed up—
my blood, my blood, my joyous blood.

Sonnet for the Changeable Body

That first year at camp, knowing that the boys
were two hundred yards away through the woods,
I often snuck out with a flashlight, stood
signalling on the knoll between, a ploy
I'd seen in countless spy movies. I learned
summer was the time to be what I wished:
bad. Nice girls didn't do it. They fished
and swam, boated and braided lanyards, spurned
the advances of tan boys at the lake
where when I touched the slippery bottom of silt
I thought of bodies—his and mine—the silk
skin beneath our clothes, hands like velvet rakes.
When my bikini line faded that fall
my old self returned: bookish, shy, too tall.

Shrunk

I consign them to a shelf—the mother
who pushed the child from her lap,
the father who administered the beatings—
the mother sprawled like a rag doll,
the father transformed into a plastic dinosaur—
T-rex, erect, with those little hands
and big teeth. The doctor locks

the door. (Her own mother is chained
to the Great Wall of China.)
It's not to make them suffer—
they've already suffered in ways I'll never know—
but to silence them.

It's good to imagine them small,
alongside Legos and fairy tale books
with children reduced to crumbs.
But what to do with the brother
and sister, not innocent, not blameless
either. I place them in the corner, their backs
to me, as in life.

There is no place among the miniatures
for the oldest child, the sister who died
at thirty-two. In photos, she is the one
who holds and rocks me, the one
in formal portraits whose hand reaches furtively
past the starched dresses and fake palms
to hold my smaller hand. Perhaps the photo followed
a beating or fight. Her arm seems impossibly long;
it seems to bend like light, to *be* light
as the hand of love would be.

Ars Poetica

Everyone here is working to embrace
randomness, to scrap easy
meaning, that limbic g-spot in the brain.
One artist has inked out letters
in a bird encyclopedia, leaving
only the scattered script of *Waiting
for Godot,* as if it had been waiting
there, encoded like DNA.

I write about the carpenter bees
that tumble through my studio, their legs
upholstered like sofas, along with the errant
stink bugs and casteneted
click beetles I've ushered outside.
Still trying to be random,
I turn to the geldings in the pasture
who've learned to come when I whistle and tsk.

A bay and a black, they like to be scratched
and nuzzle the lint in my pockets.
                              I remember
playing horses on the playground,
neighing, rearing, tossing my head,
pretending to be a stallion, not knowing
it meant a male. I wanted that noble
profile, that pennant of ripped silk

streaming across the finish line,
my father's money and hope with it.
Though he hadn't said a word
and I'd never seen one except in books,
by the age of six I already knew

there was nothing, not even his own child,
more beautiful than a horse
in motion.

The Old Empire

In sleep, I open again
the heavy, transomed door
of Latin Five. It's 1961.
Miss Virginia Quick, sponsor
of the Honor Society,
Mistress of the Punic Wars,
picks me to decline a feminine
noun. It's all I can do

to keep a straight face
above Dave Seagal whispering *All
rise for the genital case.*
Later, translating Virgil,
Miss Quick obscures a line
with *limb* for *leg* and *abdomen*
for *loins.* No use. We
sniffed the poet's lusty

bent in Book IV, when, to please
herself, not the gods,
Queen Dido "married" Aeneas
in a cave. The hair of his head
stiff as a plaster wreath,
a pincushion beard
raising roses on her shoulders
as he took her from the rear.

Miss Quick's empire rested
not on the conquest of foreign soil
by the cock, augury by entrail,
or the scrape of dagger on breast-
bone. All her *"mirabile dictu"*s

were saved for Roman laws
and plumbing, for the aqueduct
which so advanced the cause

of hygiene. I picture her now in a marble
heaven like our Congress
where petty gods squabble
and take sides. There, dressed
in the demurest toga
of the day, Virginia
Quick entertains her suitors, fetes
them with flamingo wings and dates,

brandishing her syntax
like a sword
as she flirts up a storm
in her dead language.

Painter's Whites

Always homesick for Florida,
Father called his business *Sunshine
Decorators*, the way I used to write over
and over the name of the boy
I loved. Some nights he let me
watch him stir in the tint—liquid feathers
of mint, flamingo, Prussian blue.
This was before rollers, in the days
of boar bristle and spirits
of turpentine and brushes tended
like ranch minks.

Morning brought him dazzling
from the bedroom, a man wearing pure
glare, a knife
crease in the starched trousers,
the cap's small white visor
pulled down like a frown.
Mother and I watched the brightness
leave, his ladder with its red rag
dragging from the station wagon
like the gnawed-off leg
of a trapped animal.

Honeysuckle

In October, at the end of Indian summer,
when the roses have gone
bare-hipped and the pears ripen faster
than we can eat them, and cattle
turn their haunches to the rain and the wind
takes a last audit of the trees,
leaving only turkey vultures, it is still
there, riding the fence wire, the perfume
hoarded all day by bees seeping into evening
as the light drains back into the ground.

Once I licked the trumpets' nectar,
tied the vines into garlands and rings
and pressed a pair of flowers to my chin,
rearing up with the ivory
tusks of elephants. Now, I bring
a branch inside, not because it's the only
thing in bloom. This sprig, which later
the moon will carve into shooting stars,
once belonged to a somber princess—
my drowned voice, my crown of wishes!

In the Cave

1.

I'm five and won't come out
for anyone. I know
that beyond the stilled sheet I've hung
from the piano to make my cave
terror breeds, as it does inside the closed eyes
of sleep—that nightmare
of floating off my bed
and out the window, falling up
into the sky, the stars
waiting above like broken glass.
That day I'd stood on the table
turning like a wound-down toy
while Mother hemmed my dress,
the green pincushion on her wrist plumping
into hills, the straight pins rising
in a tiny skyline, like the city
underneath me in the dream—a bright bed
of nails. Even after I opened my eyes
and crawled to their bedroom one muscle
at a time, Father continued
to sleep. Mother walked me back
without a word. All night I stared
out my window, until the sky
like some huge animal colored on its belly
for love and on its back for strife,
rolled over into day.

2.

Once I glimpsed a woman
in a cubicle at the bank
examining not the jewelry spilled
on red velvet beneath an anglepoise lamp,
but her hands, moving them in and out
of the light shaped like a furnace door
as if each finger had a story
she was incinerating. Then she clicked
off the lamp and turned her hands as slowly
as you'd turn a patient so badly burned
that even air feels sharp on the skin.

3.

The last time I fished with my father
was July. On the bayous
at sundown the water
grows dark grudgingly,
the bright discs of light
jammed like dimes
in the slots of the waves
which kept coming, like the silence
that lapped between us
all our lives and the change he chucked
on the dresser after bad nights
at the track. Now he was old
and the silence was old; it had softened
into something almost useful—

like a fishing rag, used first to clothe,
then to clean, then to hold
the fish so you don't get finned.

4.

It took him nearly a year to die.
Whenever the nurse phoned at night
she said my name like a question,
as if offering me a chance
to be somebody else. Mother,
after three strokes, could no longer
speak except to moan, though even then
I understood she was thinking
about her grief the way she thought
about her life, the way for years
I'd thought of mine *I want, I want*
what I had, no matter how bad it was.

In Late Summer

Laden with fruit, the seckle pear
begins its annual bending, the wood
at its most resilient, spongy
with summer rain. On the sleeping porch
at night I can hear the heartwood
creaking as the crown droops lower
like a fountain turned down,
so much fruit straining the tree—
pith and root, branch and leaf—
the weight of sweetness
almost as heavy as grief.

Torca

1.

Susquehanna, that was the name of the dark
swirl where they took us campers to swim,
but I told myself it was the name
a Lenape mother whispered as she brushed
her daughter's black satin hair. It was summer,
the first great sadness of my life, a homesickness
as steep as the riverbanks we clambered down.

The river was brown as tea, with mysterious hot
and cold spots. I did the dead man's float.
I opened my eyes under water to pretend
blindness. Then, because I was a child
and believed I had a place in the world, I lay
on my back and pretended to be the sky. Later,
the counselors strung a rope across and we swam
holding on through eddies that felt like drains
pulling us down.

That night, on the mattress ticked like an alley cat
I read with a flashlight under the sheets, gnawing
the jerky Mother had sent. Rhododendron
leaves scraped the cabin like rusty knives.
I pictured the willow at home lifting its arms,
sending green arrows toward our house
like a motel's VACANCY sign. Mother at the dinette,
waiting for Father's headlights to appear in the drive
like the eyes of a lost dog you've called all night.

2.

After I begged, they let me come home early.
The front door opened onto pinched
and faded rooms where words stopped and started
like tap water whenever I entered. Then Mother,
always fat, split in two, her gluttony
given a face and small clutching hands.
Did I sense my baby sister that summer
she swam inside my mother, rolled in a soft curve?

The next week, I discovered our neighbor dead
on the lawn. Sprawled in the pale swath behind
his mower, he looked relaxed, as if he'd simply
lain down on the sweet, leafy earth.
What did it mean to float as if dead and to die
as if asleep? At the river I'd watched my limbs
disappear in the murk, arms ending
at elbows, legs at knees.

That night in bed, I read as I had at camp.
But instead of a story, the print swarmed into ants.
The luminous shell-pink of my palm deepened
to red, as if the core of the earth had boiled
into my hand, turning it into flame,
into fire, into the torch I've carried
ever since, which means to suffer unrequited
love, from *torca* or *torque*—the force that comes
from something twisted.

Beauty Redux

In the forest, with its piazzas
of darkness and light,
its selvage of princely traffic;
in the forest, alias

for life, beauty becomes a woman's
name. On her hands, a muff
of glass; in the forest stew
concocted for her by eunuchs,

gristle. Meanwhile, a queen
adjusts the light on a mirror
known for ventriloquy,
its disfiguring words her own

voiced fears. The queen's love
of organ meats, the girl's
of poisonous fruit and combs—each
is deceived by the other's least

disguise. Denied the sword,
the queen wages war upon herself—
gash-red lips, eyelids colored with a bruise—
while Beauty sleeps apart

from history. For centuries the kingdom's
borders grind and snap like jaws,
coronets blare the news
of men and horses slain

and the ebony trees fray to black
threads. And if the briars soften
into tears and the little birds
must fold their wings and walk

through the diseased air?
Can anything change this spell
as long as the two are banished by a glance—
one to the forest, one to the glass—

and reveille is a kiss?

NOTES

"Pausing on a Hillside in Anatolia" is set near Izmir, Turkey.

"The Brain" is completely factual.

"The Pink Light" is for Ruth Schwartz.

"Ars Poetica" and "Letter from the Blue Ridge" are both set at the artists' colony, the Virginia Center for the Creative Arts.

ACKNOWLEDGMENTS

Thanks are due to the National Endowment for the Arts for two individual fellowships in poetry and to the Virginia Center for the Creative Arts for multiple residencies. I am grateful also to the editors of the following magazines where these poems first appeared, sometimes in provisional form or with different titles:

Alaska Quarterly Review: "Permanent Waves" and "On the Ramp of the Brooklyn Bridge" (under the title "À La Belle Étoile")

Bellevue Literary Review: "X-Ray as Credo" and "Lying in Bed, Visualizing Bone Growing"

Crab Orchard Review: "Beauty Redux"

Five Points: "Driving through the Animal"

Iluminations: "The End of the Romance" and "Milkweed"

Iron Horse Literary Review: "Honeysuckle" and "Aubade with Herons"

JAMA: Journal of the American Medical Association: "Three Disks, Two Rods and a Dozen Screws"

The Jewish Spectator: "Translation"

Kalliope: "How Could I Know" and "Torca"

Margie: "Shrunk"

New Orleans Review: "Painter's Whites"

Panhandler: "Sonnet for the Changeable Body"

Prairie Schooner: "Letter from the Blue Ridge," "Villanelle for My Two Spines," and "Pausing on a Hillside in Anatolia"

Poetry: "On St. George Island"

Southern Humanities Review: "Rara Omnia"

Southern Poetry Review: "Luminous Flux," "Funerary Tusk," and "Gowned Waiting"

Sweet: A Literary Confection: "Lightning Demonstration"

The Sow's Ear Poetry Review: "In the Cave"

The Tampa Review: "My Number"

The Women's Review of Books: "The Old Empire" and "Jazz at Bradley's"

32 Poems: "Bald"

"'Gowned Waiting'" won the 2005 Guy Owen Prize from the *Southern Poetry Review.*

"Beauty Redux" also appeared in *On the Dark Path: An Anthology of Fairy Tale Poetry* (2013).

"Permanent Waves" also appeared in the anthology *Rollins Book of Verse, 1885–2010* (Angel Alley Press, 2010.)

Seventeen of these poems appeared in the chapbook *Driving through the Animal (Floodgate Poetry Series, Volume 3.* Nashville, TN: Upper Rubber Boot Books, 2016).

ABOUT THE AUTHOR

Enid Shomer is the author of five books of poetry, two collections of short fiction and, most recently, the novel *The Twelve Rooms of the Nile*. Her poems and stories have appeared in *The New Yorker*, *The Atlantic Monthly*, *The New Criterion*, *Poetry*, *Georgia Review*, *Tikkun*, and *The Women's Review of Books*, and have been widely anthologized. In addition to fellowships in poetry from the National Endowment for the Arts and the State of Florida, her work has been honored by awards from the Poetry Society of America, *Poetry*, *Virginia Quarterly Review*, *Prairie Schooner*, and *Southern Poetry Review*.

In 2013, she received the Lifetime Achievement Award in Writing from the Florida Humanities Council.

She lives in Tampa with her husband, the painter Levent Tuncer.

ABOUT THE LEXI RUDNITSKY
EDITOR'S CHOICE AWARD

The Lexi Rudnitsky Editor's Choice Award is given annually to a poetry collection by a writer who has published at least one previous book of poems. Along with the Lexi Rudnitsky First Book Prize in Poetry, it is a collaboration of Persea Books and the Lexi Rudnitsky Poetry Project. Entry guidelines for both awards are available on Persea's website (www.perseabooks.com).

Lexi Rudnitsky (1972–2005) grew up outside of Boston, and studied at Brown University and Columbia University. Her own poems exhibit both a playful love of language and a fierce conscience. Her writing appeared in *The Antioch Review, Columbia: A Journal of Literature and Art, The Nation, The New Yorker, The Paris Review, Pequod,* and *The Western Humanities Review.* In 2004, she won the Milton Kessler Memorial Prize for Poetry from *Harpur Palate.*

Lexi died suddenly in 2005, just months after the birth of her first child and the acceptance for publication of her first book of poems, *A Doorless Knocking into Night* (Mid-List Press, 2006). The Lexi Rudnitsky book prizes were created to memorialize her by promoting the type of poet and poetry in which she so spiritedly believed.

Previous winners of the Lexi Rudnitsky Editor's Choice Award:

2018   Cameron Awkward-Rich, *Dispatch*

2017   Gary Young, *That's What I Thought*

2016   Heather Derr-Smith, *Thrust*

2015   Shane McCrae, *The Animal Too Big to Kill*

2014   Caki Wilkinson, *The Wynona Stone Poems*

2013   Michael White, *Vermeer in Hell*

2012   Mitchell L. H. Douglas, *blak al-febet*

2011   Amy Newman, *Dear Editor*